INVASIVE PLANTS OF INDIA

MANISH CHADDA

To the unsung heroes battling against nature's unwanted invaders,
the researchers, ecologists, and conservationists who tirelessly
work to protect India's rich biodiversity.

Contents

Preface

India, a land of immense biodiversity, is unfortunately grappling with the insidious threat of invasive plant species. These alien intruders, having breached our ecological boundaries, are wreaking havoc on our delicate ecosystems. This book is a comprehensive attempt to document the identity, origin, distribution, impact, and management strategies for these botanical invaders.

It is our hope that this compendium of knowledge will serve as a valuable resource for researchers, policymakers, farmers, and environmentalists. By understanding the challenges posed by these invasive plants, we can develop effective strategies to mitigate their impact and protect India's rich natural heritage.

This book is dedicated to the tireless efforts of scientists, researchers, and conservationists who are working tirelessly to combat the menace of invasive plant species in India. Their dedication inspires us all to contribute to a greener and more sustainable future.

Acknowledgements

"I extend my sincere gratitude to Shri Narsanna Kopula, the founder of Aranya Agriculture Alternatives in Zahirabad, for introducing me to the concept of allelopathy, which sparked the idea for this book."

Prologue

The Silent Invasion

India, a land of unparalleled biodiversity, is under siege. An unseen army of invaders, cloaked in green, is silently infiltrating its rich ecosystems. These are not hostile forces in the traditional sense, but rather, insidious plants that have migrated from distant lands. They arrive unnoticed, often as stowaways or ornamental imports, and once established, they spread with alarming rapidity.

With their ability to adapt, compete, and reproduce aggressively, these botanical invaders pose a formidable challenge to our delicate ecological balance. They choke our waterways, invade our farmlands, and diminish the splendor of our forests. This book is an attempt to shine a spotlight on these silent invaders, to understand their origins, their modus operandi, and the strategies to combat them. It is a call to arms for all those who cherish India's natural heritage.

CHAPTER I

An Introduction

Humans have a long history of introducing non-native species to new environments. From the earliest migrations, people carried plants and animals familiar to them from their homelands. Early European settlers in North America were particularly active in this process, intentionally introducing a wide range of agricultural and ornamental species. Over time, the focus shifted from simply transplanting familiar life forms to a deeper understanding of the ecological implications and scientific value of these non-native species.

Thriving ecosystems function like a well-oiled machine, with all organisms playing a balanced role. This intricate web of life keeps populations in check, naturally preventing any single species from becoming overly abundant or invasive. However, the introduction of non-native species by humans disrupts this equilibrium. Because ecosystems haven't evolved alongside these newcomers, they lack the natural predators or competitors to keep their populations in control. Therefore, the presence of invasive species serves as a stark reminder of the impact human activity can have on delicate ecological systems.

Healthy ecosystems strive for a balance between different species. However, this balance is dynamic, not a constant state of motion. Invasive species can disrupt this balance, exploiting niches left empty due to factors like climate change or human activity. While other external factors might play a role, human actions like transporting organisms far from their native habitat are the main cause of biological invasions.

The majority of invasive plants in South Asia arrived as decorative elements for gardens and landscapes. Others were introduced for agricultural or horticultural purposes. Some snuck in as contaminants in seeds or on transport machinery, while others hitched a ride unintentionally. While countries like Australia, New Zealand, and South Africa prioritize managing invasive plant threats, Asia tends to focus on simply describing the basic patterns of these invasions. Research efforts in Asia are also unevenly distributed, with no documented studies on invasive plants in Afghanistan or the Maldives. This lack of research and focus on management leaves most Asian countries significantly less prepared to confront new and emerging plant invasions compared to their counterparts in North America, Western Europe, and Oceania.

Among the countries is South Asia, India has the highest number of immersive plants, 145 in number and naturalized plant species 471. A species that is introduced outside of its native range due to international and unintentional human activity is considered an alien species. Alien species creating self-sustaining population in the invaded region are termed naturalized species, and a outset of naturalized species that rapidly spread in the invaded region from the site if its original introduction are considered invasive.

The socioeconomic problems caused by invasive plants are escalating on all continents. Economic costs due to biological invasions an comparably high in South Asia (US$ 185.8 billion) ($1.288 billion world wide) in between 1970 and 2017, and agriculture is the most affected section. In India alone, the estimated economic cool is US$ 176.7 billion. These costs have increased markedly in the past decades and do not show any sign of slowing down.

Managing invasive species without baseline date and their introduction pathway in difficult. These region wise on country, wire, detailed, up to date inventories of alien species are urgently needed. In fact, the impact of the environment are well document Nentwig etc dt. 2018; Langmainer and Lafain 2020) and North America (Ducnes et dt. 2018) in the Northern Hemisphare, and South Africa (van Wilgen etc. dt. 2020; McGaw at etc. 2022, Richardson et dt. 2022). New Zealand and Australia in the Southern Hemisphere.

In addition to this, several databases such as GISD (Global Invasive species Database www.iucngisd.org), GRJIS (Global Register of Introduced and Invasive Alien species; www.griis.org) CABI (Invasive species compendium; www.cabi.org/ISC), GPONAF (Global Naturalized Ambien Flora), and DAISIE (Delivering Alien species inventories for Europe), provide date for particular regions. But in India still much research individual studies documentation is required for management of invasive species.

South Asia is home to one of the Oldest civilization of the world and surrounded by the Himalayas in North and Indian Ocean is South, containing eight countries (viz. Afganistan, Bangladesh, Bhutan, India, Pakistan, Maldives, Nepal and Sri Lanka). Covers about 5.2 million Sq. Km. it is about 11.7% of the Asia continent and 3.5% of the world's land surface area. South Asia overlap with three biodiversity hotspots. They are Himalaya, Indo-Burma and Western Ghats), and harbouring 15.5% of global floral diversity (source: www.sacep.org (South Asia co-operative Environment Program). The climate of South Asia/ India varies, ranging from tropical monsoon in the South to a temperature climate in the north.

Despite, the research on invasive trees started in 1983, but till 2022, number of research articles on impact of invasive species are just 37 and on management is 33 and of all allelopathy is just 17 in number.

India harboured the highest number of invasive plant species 145 of total of 392 recorded invasive species in South Asia. In the present state of our knowledge India has about 44,500 species of plants already identified and clarified, and many more are yet to be identified, and described. This constitute Angiosperms (22,108), Gymnosperms (83), Pteridophytes (1319) Bryophytes (2.819), Lichens (3044), Fungi (15701), Algea (9.35) and Virus/Bacteria (1278), which accounts for 7 percent of the total plant species of world. About 28 percent of the Indian plants are endemic to the country. The Indian flora is mainly concentrated is three major centres of floristic diversity viz. The Himalayas, the Western Ghats and Andaman & Nicobar Islands, which as part of four of the thirty six identified, global biodiversity hotspots, viz, Himalayas, Western Ghats and Sri Lanka, Indo-Burma Sundaland (Nicobar Islands) .

India biodiversity hotspots are being increasingly fragmented not only by invasine plants but also by road, dams, plantations, and urbanization, which disrupt the complex interdepent relationship among species. This fragmentation load to reduce habitat areas, increased isolation, and adverse ecological impact, including declines in native species that required large, undisturbed habitats.

India is also known as one of the global hotspots of invasive alien. India has the largest economy and makes up more than 70% of the South-Asian economy. India boasts the most invasive and naturalized plant species in all of South Asia. This can be attributed to two factors: its vast size and its booming economy, which creates more opportunities for plants to be introduced. Interestingly, the Maldives, an island nation, has a higher proportion of invasive and naturalized plants compared to its total flora. This might be due to two reasons:

- Continuous Ocean Border: Being surrounded by ocean exposes the Maldives to a constant stream of propagules (seeds, spores, etc.) carried by currents and waves, increasing the chance of invasive plants establishing themselves.
- Island Vulnerability: Islands often lack the natural defenses present in mainland ecosystems, making them more susceptible to invasions by non-native species. On the other hand, Afghanistan has the fewest invasive and naturalized plants. While this might seem positive, it's likely due to a lack of comprehensive research in this area, rather than a true absence of the problem.

As many as 330 species are declared invasive out of more than 2,000 alien species in India and the costs of $127.3 billion as documented in the study comes from only 10 of these 330 species, making India the second topmost invasion-cost bearing country after the United States.

On study of 173 species of invasive alien plants in India, few was found to be the most worst invasive alien species, which were listed in '100 of the World's Worst Invasive Alien Species' list.. These include, such as *Alternanthera philoxeroides, Cassia uniflora, Clidemia hirta, Chromolaena odorata, Eichhornia crassipes, Lantana camara, Leucaena leucocephala, Mikania micrantha, Mimosa pigra, Pontederia crassipes, Parthenium hysterophorus, Prosopis juliflora* and *Ulex europaeus.*

Lantana camera L, is the world's worst invasive alien species, and is considered as widespread widely distributed, occurring in all South-Asian countries followed by *Pontederia craspices.* (GISD, www.iucngiod.org), *Lantana camera* is a species that is species that is wide spread in the greatest number of habitat, i.e. distributed sites, forests, forest edges, invasive habitat, pastures, and woodland.

A study on habitat fragmentation observes four major signs of fragmentation: (i) A reduction on habitat area. (ii) An increase in the number of habitat patches. (iii) A decrease in the size of these patches and (iv) An increase in the degree of their isolation.

CHAPTER II

About the Invasive Alien Species

Invasive species refer to non-native species that, when introduced to a new environment, can cause harm to the ecosystem, economy, or human health. These species often out-compete or negatively interact with native species, disrupt natural processes, and can lead to significant ecological imbalances. They can be plants, animals, fungi, or even microbes.

Key Characteristics of Invasive Alien Species

- **Non-Native Origin**: They are **not indigenous or native** to a particular place, hence known as non native species. Instead, human activities introduce invasive species to a new area either intentionally or unintentionally by agriculture, horticulture, aquaculture, pet trade, or as a result of transportation (e.g., ballast water discharge from ships).
- **Rapid Reproduction**: Invasive species often have **high reproductive rates**, allowing them to spread quickly in their new environment.
- **Lack of Predators**: They flourish due to **reduced competition and predation pressure** as they are introduced without their natural predators from their native habitat.
- **Ecological Tolerance**: A **wide range of environmental adaptability** allows them to thrive in diverse conditions, such as tolerance to extreme temperatures, pH levels, or disturbances like fire or floods, which enhances their survivability.
- **Alter Ecosystem Dynamics**: Invasive species can **alter ecosystem processes**, such as nutrient cycling and fire regimes, leading to changes in habitat structure and biodiversity.

Factors Promoting the Spread of Invasive Alien Species

- **Globalization and Increased Trade**: Globalization has led to a surge in the movement of goods and people around the world, which has allowed invasive species to easily infiltrate new ecosystems. For example, ships with ballast water can carry aquatic organisms across oceans, while planes and cars can transport insects, seeds, and other plant material unknowingly.

- **Climate Change**: Rising temperatures and shifting weather patterns create new habitats suitable for invasive species. For example, warmer winters allow insects like the Asian longhorned beetle (native to eastern Asia) to survive in colder regions, posing a threat to hardwood forests.

- **Habitat Degradation:** Construction projects, deforestation, and unsustainable land-use changes have led to the expansion of human settlements and urban areas. This disrupts and degrades native ecosystems and allows invasive species to establish themselves in disturbed habitats easily.

- **Introductions for Economic Purposes**: Some invasive species were intentionally introduced for economic reasons, such as agriculture, aquaculture, or ornamental plants. They can lead to unintended ecological consequences as the introduced species outcompete or negatively interact with native organisms.

- **Inadequate Biosecurity Measures**: Weak biosecurity measures such as inadequate inspection protocols for imported goods, ineffective quarantine practices, and insufficient regulations on the movement of potentially **invasive species** have aided their spread.

- **Lack of Awareness**: Public ignorance, inadequate management strategies, and insufficient funding and resources for research, monitoring, and eradication programs have further exacerbated the spread of invasive alien species.

Impacts of Invasive Alien Species

The introduction of invasive or **non native species** can have significant and detrimental impacts on ecosystems, biodiversity, and even human activities. They are as follows:

Ecological Impacts

- **Invasive species** outcompete native species, which leads to a **decline in their population and even species extinction.**
- Invasive plants may alter **soil composition, nutrient cycling, and fire regimes**, making it difficult for native vegetation to survive.
- Their introduction can disrupt food webs, change predator-prey relationships, and alter the flow of energy within an ecosystem. For example, **Cane toads** secrete skin with harmful bacteria, harming native predators that attempt to eat them.

Economic Impacts

- Invasive species can damage crops, trees, and livestock, leading to **food insecurity and decreased income for rural communities.**
- Some invasive species, like termites or rodents, can damage infrastructure like roads and bridges, costing millions in repairs and maintenance. For example, **Zebra mussels** attach to surfaces such as pipes or boat hulls, causing damage to infrastructure.

Health Impacts

- **Invasive species** can act as vectors for diseases like West Nile virus or Lyme disease. For example, the Giant African land snail has become a pest in agriculture, which poses a risk of transmitting diseases to humans.
- These can pollute water bodies, which, in turn, cause myriad health impacts.

Cultural and Recreational Impacts

- Invasive plants may **alter the aesthetics of landscapes, impacting recreational experiences.** This, in turn, affects the tourism sector and hence local economies that rely on this sector.

Steps taken to tackle threats of Invasive Species

There are several programs launched at the international and national levels to tackle the threats posed by invasive alien species:

Measures taken at the International Level

- **United Nations Convention on Biological Diversity (CBD – 1992):** The Convention emphasizes the need to prevent the introduction of, control, or eradicate invasive alien species that threaten ecosystems, habitats, or species.
- **Kunming-Montreal Global Biodiversity Framework (KMGBF – 2022):** It has been agreed under the UN CBD and aims to reduce the rate of introduction and establishment of **invasive alien species by at least 50% by 2030.**
- **Global Invasive Species Programme (GISP):** It supports research, capacity building, and management strategies to address invasive species issues worldwide. The Invasive Species Specialist Group (ISSG) is a global network of scientific and policy experts on **invasive species,** organized under the auspices of the Species Survival Commission (SSC) of the International Union for Conservation of Nature (IUCN).
- **International Plant Protection Convention (IPPC):** It is an intergovernmental treaty that aims to protect the world's plants, agricultural products, and natural resources from plant pests. One of its objectives is to mitigate the introduction and spread of invasive species. Various regional agreements and initiatives, such as the **European Union'sRegulation on Invasive Alien Species,** address invasive species at a regional level.

Measures taken at the National Level

- **Legal Framework:** Various laws and regulations enhanced for the conservation of biological diversity aid in the management of threats of invasive species. e.g. Biological Diversity Act of 2002, and the National Biodiversity Authority Act of 2002.

- **National Action Plan on Invasive Alien Species (NAPINVAS):** The Ministry of Environment, Forest and Climate Change (MoEFCC) launched the NAPINVAS plan, which focuses on the prevention, early detection, control, and management of invasive species.
- The **National Invasive Species Information Center (NISIC)** provides information and resources on invasive species in India.
- The **Himalayan Environmental Foundation** is working to control invasive species like Lantana camara in the Himalayas.
- The **Centre for Wildlife Studies** is studying the impacts of invasive species on Indian ecosystems.

Suggested Measures

Some of the key measures that can be taken to prevent and manage invasive alien species are:

Prevention Measures

- **Stricter regulations and protocols:** Implement and enforce strict regulations governing the import and transport of goods, including live plants and animals, and conduct a thorough ecological, economic, and social risk assessment associated with the species.
- **Biosecurity measures:** Providing training to individuals working at key entry points of ports, airports, and borders can be highly effective in intercepting invasive species before they enter a new environment.
- **Habitat restoration and conservation:** Involve local communities in habitat restoration and rehabilitate them by replanting native vegetation to promote ecosystem recovery.

Management Measures

- **Early detection and rapid response:** Early detection of new infestations is crucial for successful eradication. This, in turn, requires proper monitoring programs, surveillance networks, and public reporting systems.
- **Global Collaboration:** As the threats posed by invasive species transcend the boundaries, sharing information, resources, and expertise across borders would become essential to addressing this menace on a global scale.
- **Integrated Pest Management (IPM):** This may include biological control, chemical control, and mechanical control methods, applied in a strategic and environmentally sustainable manner.

Effective prevention and management of Invasive Alien Species is a complex and ongoing challenge. By combining diverse strategies, ongoing vigilance, research, adaptive management strategies, raising public awareness, and fostering international cooperation, we can safeguard our ecosystems and protect our livelihoods from the damaging impacts of invasive alien species.

Methods of Biological Control for Invasive Plants

Combating the Threat:

Invasive plants pose a major challenge to India's diverse ecosystems. Biological control offers a natural and sustainable approach to managing these harmful species. Here's a breakdown of the primary methods employed:

1. Utilizing Insect Herbivores:

The Workhorses: Insects are the most commonly used biological control agents in India. They often feed on specific parts of the invasive plant, hindering its growth and reproduction. Examples are

(i) **Cyrtobagous salviniae beetle:** Successfully controls the invasive aquatic weed Salvinia molesta by feeding on its fronds and inhibiting its growth.

(ii) **Potential for Lantana camara:** Research explores the use of the Hypena papalis moth to target this invasive shrub.

2. Introducing Fungal Pathogens:

- **Harnessing Nature's Defense:** Certain fungi can infect and weaken invasive plants, providing another method of control.
- **Challenges:** Selecting fungi with high host specificity (targeting only the invasive plant) can be more difficult compared to insects.

3. Utilizing Mite Predators:

- **Tiny But Mighty:** Mites can be effective against specific invasive plants by feeding on their leaves or sap, impacting their growth and health.
- **Example:** Limited use currently in India, but research is exploring potential applications.

4. The Power of Nematodes:

- **Microscopic Warriors:** Microscopic roundworms (nematodes) can parasitize the roots of invasive plants, causing damage and hindering their growth.
- **Challenges:** Soil conditions and environmental factors can influence the effectiveness of nematodes as biological control agents.

Choosing the Right Method:

- **Specificity is Key:** Selecting an agent that specifically targets the invasive plant and minimizes harm to native species is crucial.
- **Habitat Suitability:** Ensuring the chosen agent can thrive in the local environment is essential for long-term success.
- **Lifecycle Compatibility:** Matching the life cycle of the control agent with the vulnerable stages of the invasive plant can maximize effectiveness.

Beyond the Basics:

- **Combinations for Enhanced Control:** Integrating biological control with other methods like mechanical removal or controlled burning can be more effective than relying solely on one approach.
- **Importance of Research:** Continuously researching new and safe biological control agents for emerging invasive plant threats is vital.

Moving Forward:

- **Regulation and Safety:** The Directorate of Plant Protection and Quarantine (DPPQ&S) plays a crucial role in regulating the import and release of biological control agents to ensure their safety and effectiveness.
- **Collaboration is Key:** Successful implementation of biological control programs requires collaboration between research institutions, government agencies, and land managers.

Biological control is a complex but promising approach for managing invasive plants in India. Careful planning, scientific research, and responsible implementation are essential for maximizing its effectiveness and safeguarding the environment.

Mechanical Methods for Control of Invasive Plants

In the context of invasive species control, physical methods refer to manual or mechanical techniques that directly target the invasive species or its propagules (seeds, spores, etc.) These methods aim to remove, destroy, or disrupt the spread of the invasive species without relying on chemicals or biological control agents.

Here are some common physical methods used to control invasive plants

- **Manual Removal:** This involves physically pulling, digging up, or cutting down invasive plants. It's most effective for small infestations or in sensitive areas where chemical herbicides cannot be used.

- **Mechanical Removal:** This method utilizes tools and machinery to remove invasive plants on a larger scale. Examples include using mowers, brush cutters, or specialized equipment like hydro-axing (using high-pressure water to cut and remove plants).

- **Flooding and Draining:** Manipulating water levels can be an effective control method for some aquatic or wetland invasive plants. Flooding can drown the plants, while drying out wetlands can disrupt their reproductive cycles.

- **Mulching:** Applying a thick layer of organic material like wood chips or bark around desirable plants can suppress the growth of invasive plants by smothering them and blocking sunlight.

Important Considerations:

- **Effectiveness:** The effectiveness of various physical methods depends on the specific invasive species, its life cycle, and the surrounding environment.

- **Labor Intensity:** Some physical methods, like hand pulling or trapping, can be labor-intensive and may not be suitable for large-scale infestations.

- **Non-target Impacts:** Care needs to be taken to minimize the impact of physical methods on native species and the surrounding habitat.

- **Sustainability:** Physical methods may need to be repeated periodically to maintain control of invasive species populations.

Overall, physical methods offer a valuable tool for invasive species control, particularly in situations where chemical use is undesirable or impractical. However, their effectiveness often lies in their integration with other control methods for a comprehensive and sustainable management strategy.

Allelopathy: A Weapon in the Invasive Arsenal

The term allelopathy was first given by Molisch (1937), consist of two Greek words, allelon meaning 'mutual' and pathos meaning 'to suffer', harmful effects on each other . Allelopathy is a natural phenomenon in which different plant species affect the physiology of other plants existing in their vicinity, either negatively or positively. Allelopathy is defined as the adverse effect of a plant on another plant through the release of several secondary metabolites by plant parts into the soil. Allelopathy is a useful mechanism for alien plant invasion. Chemical exudates released from roots and other plant parts play crucial role which arbitrate mutualistic, competitive and pathogenic effects on native flora.

Allelopathy, the ability of a plant to release chemicals that inhibit the growth of others, is a key factor in the success of many invasive species, including water hyacinth. A wide variety of these chemicals have been identified in plants, such as water hyacinth, with organic acids, terpenoids, and phenols being particularly common.

These chemicals have multiple harmful effects on neighboring plants. They can disrupt essential processes like cell division, photosynthesis, and nutrient uptake. Additionally, they can alter the permeability of cell membranes and inactivate vital hormones and enzymes.

The impact extends beyond individual plants. Allelopathic substances released by water hyacinth can also harm soil microbes, disrupting the delicate balance of the soil ecosystem. This further weakens the ability of native plants to compete and survive.

In essence, allelopathy provides water hyacinth with a chemical arsenal that allows it to suppress competitors, establish dominance, and ultimately thrive in its invaded environment.

Becoming an Invader: How Plants Take Over New Homes

For a plant to successfully invade a new habitat, it needs to be tough. It has to overcome challenges in its new environment (adversities) and compete with the plants already there (native plants). The key to success lies in being adaptable and flexible (wide adaptability and physiological plasticity).

Dodging Enemies, Finding Friends: Strategies for Invasion

One way plants become invasive is by escaping their natural enemies. The enemy release hypothesis suggests that invasive plants are less likely to be eaten by herbivores or infected by diseases (pathogens) in their new home. This allows them to grow in large numbers and spread widely.

Another strategy is finding new friends. The mutualist facilitation hypothesis proposes that invasive plants can benefit from forming partnerships with new helpful organisms (mutualist species) not present in their original habitat. These new allies, like pollinators that help spread seeds or fungi that provide nutrients, can aid the invaders in establishing themselves and taking over.

Empty Niche Advantage and Chemical Warfare

Sometimes, invasive plants succeed by finding unused resources in a new environment. The Eltonian empty niche hypothesis suggests that these plants simply fill a vacant spot in the ecosystem (empty niche) where no other plant thrives.

Finally, some invasive plants have a secret weapon: unique chemical compounds. The novel weapon hypothesis explains that these plants release chemicals (allelopathic effects) that harm native plants and soil microbes. Since the native organisms haven't encountered these chemicals before, they have no defense, giving the invasive plant an advantage in the competition for space and resources.

By understanding these different strategies, we can better understand how plants become invasive and develop strategies to control their spread.

These plants have become invasive in India due to factors such as their ability to outcompete native species, adapt to various environmental conditions, and lack of natural predators or controls in their new habitats.

Sl.	Invasive Plant	Origin	Description	Invasive Characteristics	Common Name
1	*Lantana (Lantana camara)*	Central and South America	This flowering shrub is native to South America and Central America. It is now widespread in India and can be found in forests, grasslands, wastelands, and even roadsides. Lantana camara forms dense thickets that can crowd out native plants.	Forms dense thickets, displaces native vegetation, and reduces biodiversity.	Wild sage, Raimuniya, Putush, Kongini, wild-sage
2	*Parthenium (Parthenium hysterophorus)*	Central America	This fast-growing annual herb is native to tropical America. Introduced as a contaminant of crop seeds, Parthenium hysterophorus is now widespread in India. It can cause skin irritation and respiratory problems in humans and animals.	Highly allergenic pollen, reduces crop yields, and negatively impacts human health and biodiversity.	Carrot grass, Congress grass or Gajar ghas or Dhanura.
3	*Mikania (Mikania micrantha)*	Central and South America	This is a rapidly spreading vine, is a notorious invasive weed that smothers native vegetation and disrupts ecosystems.	Smothers native vegetation by forming dense mats, affecting forest regeneration and biodiversity.	Bitter vine, Climbing hemp vine, or American rope
4	*Prosopis species (Prosopis juliflora, Prosopis glandulosa)*	South America	This thorny shrub or tree is native to Central and South America, the Caribbean Islands, and Mexico. Introduced to India as a source of fuelwood and fodder, Prosopis juliflora has become invasive in many parts of the country. It displaces native vegetation and can reduce water availability.	Rapid spread in arid and semi-arid regions, outcompeting native plants and affecting local biodiversity.	Angaraji babul, Kabuli kikar, Vilayati babul, Vilayati khejra or Vilayati kikar

Sl.	Invasive Plant	Origin	Description	Invasive Characteristics	Common Name
5	*Eupatorium species (e.g., Eupatorium odoratum)*	Tropical Americas	Eupatorium species, including the notorious Chromolaena odorata (Siam weed), are invasive plants known for their rapid growth, allelopathic effects, and significant ecological damage.	Forms dense thickets, displaces native flora, and alters habitats.	Siam Weed, Bitter bush, turpentine weed, Devilweed, Hagonoy, Jack in the bush, Triffid weed.Buti patti.
6	*Water hyacinth (Eichhornia crassipes)*	South America	Water hyacinth (Eichhornia crassipes) is a rapidly spreading aquatic weed notorious for clogging waterways.	Rapid growth in water bodies, leading to clogging of waterways, impacting aquatic ecosystems and fisheries.	Water hyacinths, Terror of Bengal.
7	*Chromolaena (Chromolaena odorata)*	Tropical Americas	Chromolaena is a genus of fast-growing plants, notorious for its invasive species like Siam weed, which forms dense thickets, outcompetes native vegetation, and disrupts ecosystems.	Fast-growing shrub that forms dense thickets, displaces native vegetation, and alters ecosystem dynamics.	Bitter Bush, Chritsmas Bush, Common Floss Flower, Siam weed, Assam pacha, Communist-pacha (Malayalam) Kampurodda (Telugu)
8	*Mimosa pudica*	South America	Mimosa pudica, the famously touch-sensitive plant, is a rapid invader with a hidden aggressive side.	Mimosa pudica, a rapid-growing, invasive weed known for its sensitive leaves, forms dense mats, outcompetes native plants, and produces allelopathic chemicals.	Sensitive plant, Action plant, Humble plant, Shameplant, and Touch-me-not, Lajwanti
9	*Eucalyptus globulus Labill.*	Australia, Tasmania, and nearby islands.	A fast-growing tree with aromatic leaves, often invasive but valued for its timber and oil.	Eucalyptus is a fast-growing, water-intensive tree with allelopathic properties, often becoming an invasive species that disrupts ecosystems and depletes resources.	Tailapatra, Sugandhapatra, Tailaprana, and Nilgiri Taila

Table 1 : Some examples of invasive plants in India

These are just a few examples of the many invasive plants found in India. Invasive plants can have a serious negative impact on India's native ecosystems, agriculture, and human health.

Tropical forests are the richest biodiversity hotspots and are under immense natural and anthropogenic pressures that lead to biodiversity loss. One such cause is alien plant invasion that alters the native forest stand structure and composition and disrupts the vital ecosystem functions. Central India, which mainly spans across the three states, viz. Madhya Pradesh, Chhattisgarh and some parts of Maharashtra, is well-known for its sprawling tropical deciduous forests, which are also no less immune to the present-day pressures, including the plant invasion. Alien invasive plants arrive via several pathways and possess unique traits that help them to surpass the barriers in the new habitats, where many influential factors might operate upon them. Once established, they may profoundly impact the invaded ecosystem. Most of the studies from Central India have been focused on floristics, forest structure, impact of disturbances, etc., and relatively few studies have addressed plant invasion. Overall, there are 179 invasive taxa in Central India, mostly from the Asteraceae (17.3%) and Fabaceae (14.5%) families. Majority of them are from Tropical America (52%), and most are herbs (69%).

There are eight invasive species that are reported to reduce the productivity of agricultural fields, They are *Prosopis juliflora, Parthenium hysterophorus, Mimosa pigra, Mimosa pigra, Mikania micrantha, Lanatana camara, Bidens pilosa, Alternanthera philoxeroides & Ageratina adenophora*. There are also eight species that reported to alter soil properties viz. *Ulex europaeus, Prosopis juliflora, Parthenium hysterophorus, Lanatana camara, Clidemia hirta, Chromolaena odorata, Ageratina adenophora and Acacia mangium*. Hence, they directly affect the economy. *Clidemia hirta, Lantana camara, Leucaena leucocephala, Mikania micrantha, Parthenium hysterophorus,* and *Prosopis juliflora* were reported to affect livestock and their products. Species like *Alternanthera philoxeroides, Gymnocoronis spilanthoides, Myriophyllum aquaticum,* and *Ulex europaeus* are responsible for hydrological changes that subsequently affect aquatic ecosystems. Only two invasive plants, *Chromolaena odorata and Parthenium hysterophorus* are reported to have an impact on human health.

An invasive species are introduced as an alien, exotic, and non-indigenous species non-native to that location but very aggressive, leading to damage to the other plant species, human health and economic structure, or the organisms from their native place immigrating to a new locality are referred as exotic species. Due to enormous growth of invasive exotic species, India is facing significant environmental as well as economic problems. In India, about 42% of the weeds in crop fields are aliens. It is estimated that alien weeds have caused a 30% loss in crop production. In a study of the invasive alien flora in Uttar Pradesh, India comprises of 44 families including 109 genera and 152 species. The most common exotic species of India which has been discussed include *Ageratum conyzoides, Eupatorium adenophorum, Parthenium hysterophorus, Lantana camara, Mikania micarantha, Argemone mexicana* and *Eichhornia crassipes* (aquatic plant). Among which *Lantana camara, Parthenium hysterophorus,* and *Ageratum conyzoides* are the worst, highly invasive and challenging.

CHAPTER III

Lantana Camara: A Beautiful Invader

Lantana Camara

Lantana camara, a native of tropical and subtropical America, is unfortunately one of the world's worst invasive weeds. It was introduced to India as an ornamental plant around 1810, but things took a turn. Now, lantana is found all over India, from the foothills of the Himalayas all the way south.

This fast-spreading plant thrives on human activity. Cultivation, road construction, and deforestation create disturbed environments, perfect for lantana to take hold. Scientists have identified several reasons why lantana is such a successful invader:

- **Adaptable and Tough:** Lantana can adjust to different conditions (phenotypic plasticity) and maintain its health (fitness homeostasis).
- **Spreading Like Wildfire:** It reproduces easily through both seeds and vegetative means (stem cuttings) and can even benefit from disturbances like grazing animals (destructive foraging activities).
- **Dominating the Competition:** Lantana's wide range, fire resistance, and ability to compete aggressively for resources give it a significant edge.
- **Chemical Warfare:** Lantana releases chemicals (allelopathy) that harm other plants, further clearing the way for its dominance.

Interestingly, Lantana doesn't conquer an area all at once. It starts by rapidly establishing itself above ground with less investment in roots (low biomass allocation). This allows it to quickly cover disturbed areas with shallow, eroded soil thanks to its efficient nutrient uptake.

Lantana camara isn't just a fast-spreading weed; it has a secret weapon: chemicals! Studies have identified various compounds in lantana, like salicylic acid and coumarin, that act as allelopathic agents. These chemicals harm the growth and survival of other plants around it.

The allelopathic effect isn't limited to just slowing down other plants. Some allelochemicals in lantana's leaves, like *lantadene A* and *B*, are even toxic. Other studies have found additional allelopathic compounds in both the leaves and roots of lantana.

The impact of these chemicals is clear. Increased lantana density in forests is linked to a decline in the variety of other plant species

(species richness). This is because the allelochemicals weaken native plants, leading to lower productivity and making it harder for them to compete with lantana.

The threat goes beyond competition. Research suggests allelochemicals might contribute to wildfires in some forest areas. Additionally, lantana leaf extracts have been shown to hinder the growth of water hyacinth and commercially important crops like tomatoes and cucumbers. Lantana's allelopathic effects extend even further, inhibiting the germination and growth of other terrestrial plants through chemicals released from stems, leaves, and fruits.

In simpler terms, lantana uses a cocktail of chemicals to weaken and suppress other plants, allowing it to dominate the environment. Understanding these allelopathic effects is crucial for developing strategies to control the spread of this invasive weed.

However, research suggests that lantana's presence might not significantly impact the diversity of trees and shrubs in certain ecosystems. A study in Karnataka, India, found no major changes in tree, shrub, and herb diversity except for a decrease in herb species richness in moist deciduous forests. This suggests that the impact of lantana might vary depending on the specific environment.

CHAPTER IV

Eupatorium adenophorum (Crofton Weed): An Invasive Threat

Crofton Weed

Crofton weed, also known as *Eupatorium adenophorum*, is a nasty invasive species native to Central America. This fast-spreading weed has a branching stem and thrives under specific conditions. Its success as an invader depends on several factors, including humidity, light availability, the surrounding ecosystem, and the existing plant diversity.

One key weapon in crofton weed's arsenal is Allelopathy. Allelopathy refers to the process where plants release chemicals that harm other plants around them. Studies have identified and isolated various allelopathic compounds from crofton weed.

The essential oil of the weed contains a mix of chemicals, including *1-methyl-2(1-methyl) benzene, hedycaryol*, and *cetral*. Additionally, research by Ding et al. (1999) found a specific compound called euprtoranolide, a sesquiterpene lactone, in the flowers of E. adenophorum.

These allelopathic chemicals likely play a significant role in how crofton weed invades new areas. Understanding these compounds and their effects is crucial for developing strategies to control the spread of this invasive plant.

A major reason for crofton weed's successful invasion is its harmful effect on surrounding plants, known as allelopathy. This weed releases chemicals that act like a toxin, hindering the germination of seeds in several commercially important crops like clover, ryegrass, and corn.

These allelopathic chemicals aren't just disruptive; they can be damaging. Studies by Zhang et al. (1993) found that crofton weed leachate (liquid extract) not only affects the growth of corn but also causes physical abnormalities in its roots.

Research by Baruah et al. (1994) further explored this allelopathic effect. They used extracts from the above-ground parts of crofton weed and identified specific chemicals called *cadinenes* and *β-sitosterol*. These chemicals were then tested on seeds of onion (*Allium cepa*), radish (*Raphanus sativus*), and cucumber (*Cucumis sativus*), and their germination was negatively impacted.

In essence, crofton weed uses a chemical warfare strategy to weaken and suppress the growth of neighboring plants, making it easier for the weed to establish itself and dominate the environment. This allelopathic effect poses a significant threat to agriculture and highlights the need for control measures.

CHAPTER V

Parthenium Weed (Congress Grass): A Growing Threat in India

Parthenium Weed

The Parthenium weed (*Parthenium hysterophorus L.*) was a topic of concern at a recent conference. This aggressive invader, native to tropical America, has taken root in most parts of India due to its ability to spread rapidly.

First spotted in Maharashtra in 1951, Parthenium thrives in disturbed areas with exposed soil, like fallow lands, roadsides, and overgrazed pastures. It usually struggles to establish itself in areas with healthy existing vegetation.

This fast-growing weed has earned its reputation as a noxious one for several reasons:

- **Prolific Seeding and Spread:** Parthenium produces a vast amount of seeds, allowing it to quickly take over new areas.

- **Allelopathic Effects:** It releases chemicals that harm other plants, giving it a competitive advantage.
- **Crop Competition:** Parthenium aggressively competes with crops for resources, impacting agricultural yields.
- **Health Hazards:** This weed is highly allergenic, causing breathing problems, skin irritation (dermatitis), and asthma in humans and animals.

Despite these known issues, research on Parthenium's impact on overall ecosystems is limited, particularly regarding its allelopathic effects and interactions with crops.

One study by A.S. Raghubanshi et al. investigated the weed's influence on soil nutrients and processes in agricultural ecosystems. This research highlights the importance of considering factors like sampling time and season when studying invasive species. The study concludes that long-term monitoring is crucial to fully understand the long-term consequences of invasive species like Parthenium weed on ecosystems.

Parthenium weed (*Parthenium hysterophorus*) is a nightmarish weed for wastelands and other disturbed areas. This has led to a large-scale invasion. Parthenium started in the hilly regions of India but has since spread to lower areas, engulfing most of the country (Dogra et al. 2009). Over the past two decades, it's become a common weed in both urban and natural habitats, pushing out native plant species.

Chemical Warfare: Allelopathy

One major reason for Parthenium's success is allelopathy. The weed releases chemicals (phenolic compounds like o-coumaric acid and sesquiterpene lactones) that harm other plants. These chemicals are like a one-two punch:

- **Native plants are not used to these chemicals** and struggle to survive or grow properly, leading to a decline in their population.

- **Soil microbes can't break down these allelochemicals** (Callaway & Aschehoug 2000), further hindering the growth of other plants.

Impact Beyond Plants

Parthenium doesn't just harm other plants; it poses a health threat to humans and animals. The pollen and dust from the weed can cause allergic skin reactions (dermatitis). These allergic reactions are linked to the cytotoxic (poisonous to cells) nature of the sesquiterpene lactones released by the weed. In severe cases, exposure to Parthenium can lead to diarrhea, breathlessness, and even choking.

Parthenium weed is a serious ecological and health concern in India. Understanding its aggressive strategies and harmful effects is crucial for developing effective control measures.

Essential oil of Eucalyptus has potential to control Parthenium hysterophorus

CHAPTER VI

Mikania micrantha: A Growing Threat in Indian Forests

Mikania Micrantha

A study by K.V. Sankaran and M.A. Sreenivasan (Kerala Forest Research Institute) highlighted the alarming spread of *Mikania micrantha*, a fast-growing invasive weed of Neotropical origin. This aggressive plant is becoming a major threat to natural forests, plantations, and agricultural systems in northeast and southwest India.

The presentation focused on the negative impacts of *Mikania micrantha*, including:

- **Reduced Crop Yields:** The weed's presence significantly reduces crop yields.
- **Loss of Biodiversity:***Mikania micrantha* disrupts the natural balance, leading to a decline in native plant diversity.
- **Hindered Forest Regeneration:** The weed's rapid growth prevents the natural regeneration of trees in forests.

The study revealed that over 60% of surveyed locations showed varying degrees of infestation by *Mikania micrantha*. These infestations were primarily found in moist deciduous forests, teak plantations, and disturbed forest areas. The presentation also discussed potential control methods for this invasive weed.

Mikania micrantha, a fast-growing perennial vine with tiny flowers, is no friend to gardens or forests. This aggressive weed, also known as the "plant killer" or "mile-a-minute vine," is native to the Neotropics. Ironically, it was introduced to India during World War II for camouflage purposes. Today, it's a major problem in natural habitats and agricultural areas across North-East India, blanketing most of Asia from Sri Lanka to Bangladesh.

Studies by Raghubanshi et al. (2005) found that over 60% of forests, teak plantations, and disturbed areas in North-East India are infested by Mikania micrantha. This aggressive vine climbs readily on both small and tall trees, smothering their foliage. It's considered one of the world's worst weeds due to its:

- **Rapid Reproduction:** Mikania boasts a remarkable reproductive capacity, spreading not just through seeds but also vegetatively through plant debris and underground roots .
- **Chemical Warfare:** The plant utilizes allelopathy, releasing chemicals (including mikanin, eupafolin, and volatile oils) that harm other plants around it. These allelopathic effects have been shown to inhibit the growth of various crops like radish, ryegrass, and clover, and even reduce the biomass of tomatoes and legumes.

Mikania micrantha's aggressive growth and allelopathic properties pose a significant threat to North-East India's natural ecosystems and agricultural productivity. Understanding its impact and developing effective control measures are crucial to protect the region's biodiversity and agricultural yields.

CHAPTER VII

Prosopis juliflora: From Helpful Introduction to Invasive Threat

Prosopis juliflora

Prosopis juliflora, a thorny tree or shrub native to the hot, dry regions of the West Indies, Mexico, and Central and South America, has a complex history in India. While there are two *Prosopis* species in India, *P. cineraria* is native, while *P. juliflora* became a major invasive problem.

Introduced in the late 19th century with good intentions:

- **Green Dreams:***P. juliflora* was brought in to help control desertification and beautify landscapes in arid regions.
- **Fuelwood Solution:** It was also seen as a potential source of firewood, easing pressure on natural forests.

However, things took a turn for the worse:

- **Aggressive Invader:** Unfortunately, *P. juliflora* proved to be a highly aggressive weed. It escaped plantations and outcompeted native plants.
- **National Threat:** Today, it's a major invasive species across India, suppressing native vegetation. Similar problems have been reported in other parts of the world.

The unintended consequences of introducing *P. juliflora* are evident:

- **Forest Takeover:** The weed forms dense stands, pushing out native plants in forests, wastelands, and even croplands.
- **Fuelwood Paradox:** While introduced for fuelwood, its dense growth can hinder access to firewood for local communities.

Prosopis juliflora can have both positive and negative impacts on the environment it's introduced to. While it may offer some benefits to soil fertility, these are often outweighed by the harmful effects it has on surrounding plant life.

Positive Effects:

- Studies like one by El-Keblawy and Abdelfatah (2013) suggest that *P. juliflora* can increase essential nutrients (potassium, nitrogen, and phosphorus) in the soil. Additionally, it can contribute to higher organic matter content, which improves water retention and soil texture.

Negative Effects:

- Research by Kaur et al. (2012) in India found that *P. juliflora* can create "resource islands" by concentrating organic nitrogen and carbon around its roots. However, the allelopathic chemicals it releases ultimately overpower these benefits. Allelopathy refers to the process where plants release chemicals that harm the growth of other plants.

Prosopis juliflora: A Threat to Arid Ecosystems

Prosopis juliflora is spreading rapidly in arid and hyper-arid regions, posing a significant threat to native plant diversity and overall ecosystem health. This invasive tree disrupts the natural balance in several ways:

- **Reduced Abundance and Richness:***P. juliflora* discourages the growth and presence of many native plant species, leading to a decline in overall plant variety and abundance.
- **Dominant Stands:***P. juliflora* often forms dense, single-species clusters, preventing other plants from growing beneath or around its canopy.
- **Shifting Dynamics:** While studies suggest P. juliflora can be beneficial in its native range (Tiedemann and Klemmedson 1973; Kaur et al. 2012), its behavior changes dramatically when introduced to new environments. In invaded areas, the understory (plant life below the main canopy) has far fewer species compared to areas with native trees (Aggarwal et al. 1976).

Negative Impacts Beyond the Canopy

Research in the Arabian Peninsula highlights the severity of the problem. While *P. juliflora* may increase some nutrients in the soil beneath its canopy, it has a strong negative impact on native plant communities (El-Keblawy and Al-Rawai 2007). This negative effect extends beyond the area directly shaded by the canopy, especially in dense stands. Studies show that older and denser *P. juliflora* sites have significantly lower plant density, frequency, and diversity, particularly for annual species.

P. juliflora might offer some initial advantages for soil nutrients, the allelopathic effects it has on surrounding vegetation outweigh these benefits. This highlights the complex and sometimes contradictory consequences of introducing non-native species to new environments.

CHAPTER VIII

Water Hyacinth (Eichhornia crassipes): A Rapid Invader

Water Hyacinth

Water hyacinth, scientifically known as *Eichhornia crassipes*, is a notorious aquatic weed originally from South America. Renowned for its rapid growth and ability to spread aggressively, it has become a significant problem in many parts of the world, including India.

This floating plant reproduces primarily through runners (stolons), allowing it to quickly form dense mats on the water's surface. Its success as an invader is attributed to its adaptability to different environments and its ability to outcompete native plants.

Introduced to many countries for ornamental purposes or to purify water bodies, water hyacinth has now become a major nuisance, clogging waterways, hindering navigation, and disrupting aquatic ecosystems. In India, it was introduced around 1914-1916 and has since spread widely.

These dense mats of water hyacinth block sunlight from reaching underwater plants, reduce oxygen levels in the water, and disrupt aquatic life. Additionally, the weed can also harbor disease-carrying organisms.

The rapid growth and spread of water hyacinth pose a significant challenge to water management and ecosystem health worldwide.

Water hyacinth (*Eichhornia crassipes*) isn't just a nuisance due to its rapid growth; it also employs chemical warfare. Research has identified several compounds within this plant, including *linoleic* acid, *glycerol-1,9-12 (ZZ)-octa decadienoic* acid, and *N-phenyl-2-napthylamine* .

Of particular interest is *N-phenyl-2-napthylamine,* which has been shown to inhibit the growth of various aquatic plants. It can even alter the protein content and antioxidant levels in some aquatic organisms.

The water surrounding water hyacinth itself can be harmful to other plants. Studies have shown that water where water hyacinth grows can hinder the growth of algae, even outperforming traditional algaecides like copper sulfate.

These chemical defenses give water hyacinth a significant advantage over other aquatic plants, contributing to its dominance in water bodies.

Despite its reputation as a pesky invasive species, the water hyacinth possesses a surprising ability to clean polluted water. These aquatic plants act as natural filters, absorbing excess nutrients like nitrogen and phosphorus from sewage. They can even break down certain contaminants found in wastewater. This natural filtration process offers a potential solution for wastewater treatment, though it's essential to manage their growth carefully due to their rapid proliferation, which can clog waterways and disrupt ecosystems.

CHAPTER IX

Chromolaena odorata: An Invasive Menace

Chromolaena odorata

Chromolaena odorata, commonly known as Siam weed, is a rapidly proliferating invasive plant species native to tropical America. This herbaceous weed has become a significant ecological and agricultural problem in various parts of the world, including India, Southeast Asia, and Africa. Its aggressive nature, coupled with its allelopathic potential, has made it a challenging species to control.

Native to tropical and subtropical regions of Central and South America, Chromolaena odorata was introduced to many parts of the world, including Asia, Africa, and Australia, as an ornamental plant or accidentally as a contaminant in agricultural products. Its ability to thrive in diverse ecological conditions and its prolific seed production have contributed to its rapid spread and establishment in new environments. Viogt in 1845 reported that Chromolaena odorata was introduced to Calcutta Botanical Garden in India as an ornamental plant. Clarke in 1876 mentioned it had become wild in parts of India and Java.

One of the primary factors contributing to the invasive success of *Chromolaena odorata* is its allelopathic potential. Allelopathy refers to the chemical interaction between plants, where one plant produces substances that inhibit the growth of others. Studies have shown that *Chromolaena odorata* releases allelochemicals that adversely affect the germination and growth of several plant species ' . These allelochemicals can suppress the growth of both agricultural crops and native vegetation, leading to a decline in biodiversity and productivity.

The invasion of *Chromolaena odorata* has far-reaching ecological consequences. It forms dense stands that outcompete native vegetation, leading to a reduction in species richness and diversity. Moreover, its rapid growth and spread can disrupt ecosystem processes, such as nutrient cycling and hydrological regimes. By altering the microclimate and soil properties, Chromolaena odorata can create conditions that favor its own survival and further inhibit the establishment of native species.

Management Strategies

Controlling *Chromolaena odorata* requires a multi-faceted approach that combines various management techniques. Some of the commonly used methods include:

Physical Control: Manual uprooting, mowing, and cutting can be effective for small-scale infestations. However, these methods are labor-intensive and often require repeated applications.

Chemical Control: Herbicides can be used to control large-scale infestations, but their indiscriminate nature can harm non-target organisms and contaminate the environment.

Biological Control: The introduction of natural enemies, such as insects or pathogens, can provide a long-term solution for managing Chromolaena odorata. However, careful evaluation and risk assessment are essential to prevent unintended consequences. Pareuchaetes pseudoinsulata, a moth, was introduced to India in 1973 under Commonwealth Institute of Biological Control (CIBC, now CABI Bioscience) as one of the first natural enemy identified.

Integrated Weed Management (IWM): Combining multiple control methods is often the most effective approach. IWM involves the strategic use of physical, chemical, and biological control techniques in conjunction with preventive measures to minimize the impact of *Chromolaena odorata* on the environment.

Chromolaena odorata poses a significant threat to biodiversity and ecosystem health. Its ability to rapidly invade and dominate disturbed areas, coupled with its allelopathic potential, makes it a challenging weed to control. Effective management requires a comprehensive approach that considers the specific ecological context and the available resources. Continued research and development of innovative control strategies are essential to mitigate the negative impacts of this invasive species.

CHAPTER X

Ageratum conyzoides: A Troublesome Weed

Ageratum Conyzoides

Ageratum conyzoides are the worst, highly invasive and challenging. *Ageratum conyzoides*, commonly known as billy goat weed or tropical white weed, is a highly invasive plant native to tropical regions. It has successfully colonized various habitats worldwide, including roadsides, fields, and agricultural areas. This aggressive weed is known for its rapid spread, facilitated by its ability to produce thousands of long-lived seeds.

One of the primary reasons for its invasive success is its allelopathic nature. This means it releases chemicals that inhibit the growth of other plants. Compounds like *ageratochromene, precocene I*, and *precocene II*, found in *Ageratum*, have been identified as having herbicidal properties. These chemicals interfere with the growth and development of neighboring plants, reducing crop yields and disrupting natural ecosystems.

In agricultural settings, *Ageratum conyzoides* is a particularly troublesome weed, causing significant losses in staple crops like wheat, corn, and rice. Its ability to thrive in diverse environments, combined with its aggressive growth and allelopathic effects, makes it a challenging weed to control.

The problem is exacerbated by the plant's ability to reproduce both sexually (through seeds) and asexually (through stolons). This dual reproductive strategy allows it to rapidly colonize new areas and establish persistent populations.

CHAPTER XI

The Touch-Me-Not Plant: A Delicate Invader

Touch-Me-Not

Mimosa pudica, commonly known as the touch-me-not plant or sensitive plant, is a fascinating yet problematic species. Native to tropical South America, it has spread globally due to its unique characteristics and has become an invasive weed in many regions.

The touch-me-not plant, *Mimosa pudica,* is renowned for its rapid leaf folding response to touch. While this characteristic makes it a fascinating subject for observation, it has also contributed to its invasive success. Beyond its unique sensitivity, this plant possesses traits that enable it to outcompete native vegetation. *Mimosa pudica* is an aggressive colonizer, forming dense mats that suppress the growth of other plants. It has been discovered that this plant produces chemicals known as allelopathic compounds, which inhibit the growth of neighboring species. This chemical warfare, combined with its rapid growth and prolific seed production, allows

Mimosa pudica to dominate disturbed areas and displace native flora.

This plant's ability to form dense mats, combined with its sensitivity to touch, allows it to outcompete native vegetation and disrupt ecological balance. Its seeds are easily dispersed, enabling it to colonize new areas rapidly. Additionally, *Mimosa pudica* produces chemicals that inhibit the growth of other plants, further solidifying its dominance in disturbed environments.

While the plant's sensitivity and rapid movement are intriguing, its invasive nature poses a significant threat to biodiversity and agricultural practices in various parts of the world.

Manual Control: Although the thorns make hand pulling unpleasant, the plant can be controlled by hoeing. Cultivation can also held keep the plant under control.

Biological Control: Are often found attacked by a fungus Ramularia mimosae, which grows on the upper surface of the leaflets, forming irregular white spots.

Chemical Control: Foliar treatment (wetting must be through): 2,4,5-T (1 kg/500 l, spot-spraying, 500 g/ha, Jamaica, grassland, 3 kg/ha, Malaysia, rubber) amitrole (4.5 kg/ha, Ceylon, Tea), picloram (pasture), ametryne (cane), fenoprop, ioxynil plus 2,4 D.

CHAPTER XII

Eucalyptus: A Double-Edged Sword

Eucalyptus

Eucalyptus, a genus of flowering trees and shrubs belonging to the *Myrtaceae* family, is native to Australia and Tasmania. Characterized by their distinctive aromatic leaves and rapid growth, eucalyptus species have been widely introduced to various parts of the world for a multitude of purposes.

The introduction of eucalyptus to regions outside its native range began in the 19th century. These trees were initially prized for their timber, pulpwood, and essential oils. Their fast growth and ability to thrive in diverse climatic conditions made them attractive for afforestation and soil conservation efforts.

Eucalyptus trees were first introduced outside their native range in the early 19th century. European settlers and colonial botanists recognized the trees' potential for timber, fuel, and medicinal purposes. They were planted in many countries, including the United States, South Africa, and parts of South America. The initial enthusiasm for eucalyptus was driven by its rapid growth and adaptability to various climates, but this quickly gave way to concerns as the trees began to show their invasive tendencies.

Eucalyptus as an Invasive Species

While eucalyptus has been a valuable resource in some contexts, its introduction to certain ecosystems has had detrimental consequences. In many regions, it has been classified as an invasive species due to its aggressive growth, ability to outcompete native vegetation, and negative impacts on soil and water resources.

One of the primary concerns with eucalyptus is its water consumption. Known for its high transpiration rates, it can significantly deplete groundwater levels, leading to water scarcity issues in arid and semi-arid regions. Moreover, its dense canopy creates a shaded environment that inhibits the growth of understory vegetation, reducing biodiversity and altering ecosystem processes.

Eucalyptus plantations can also contribute to soil acidification. The decomposition of eucalyptus leaves produces acidic compounds that can lower soil pH, affecting the availability of essential nutrients for other plant species. This can further disrupt the ecological balance and reduce the overall productivity of the land.

Allelopathic Effects of Eucalyptus

Allelopathy, the chemical inhibition of the growth of other plants, is another factor contributing to the invasive nature of eucalyptus. Studies have shown that eucalyptus leaves and litter contain allelopathic compounds that can suppress the germination and growth of neighboring plants. These chemicals can leach into the soil, affecting soil microbial communities and creating a hostile environment for other species.

The allelopathic potential of eucalyptus has been linked to the formation of monocultures, where the species dominates the landscape to the exclusion of other plants. This reduction in plant diversity can have cascading effects on the ecosystem, impacting wildlife, pollinators, and other organisms that rely on a diverse plant community.

Ecological Allotropic Effects

Allelopathy: Eucalyptus leaves release allelopathic chemicals into the soil, which can inhibit the growth of other plants. These chemicals, such as cineole and other terpenes, can create a hostile environment for native flora, further promoting the dominance of eucalyptus.

Soil Composition: The decomposition of eucalyptus leaves and bark can alter soil pH and nutrient composition. The high acidity and the presence of certain chemical compounds can affect the growth of other plant species and the microbial communities within the soil.

Health-Related Allotropic Effects

Air Quality: Eucalyptus trees emit volatile organic compounds (VOCs) into the atmosphere. While some VOCs have medicinal properties and are used in essential oils, they can also contribute to air pollution. In areas with high eucalyptus density, the concentration of these compounds can impact air quality, potentially exacerbating respiratory conditions.

Human Health: Prolonged exposure to eucalyptus oils and dust from the trees can cause respiratory irritation in sensitive individuals. Allergic reactions, including skin rashes and respiratory issues, have been reported in some cases.

Ecological Impact

Biodiversity Loss:

Eucalyptus trees can outcompete native vegetation for resources such as water, light, and nutrients. Their dominance can lead to the decline of native plant species and disrupt local wildlife habitats. In some regions, eucalyptus forests have replaced diverse native ecosystems, leading to reduced biodiversity.

Negative Impacts on Biodiversity

- **Reduced Understory Vegetation:** Eucalyptus trees often create dense canopies that block sunlight, inhibiting the growth of understory plants. This reduction in plant diversity can have cascading effects on the entire ecosystem, affecting herbivores, insects, and other organisms dependent on understory vegetation.

- **Soil Acidification:** The decomposition of eucalyptus leaves can acidify the soil, making it less suitable for a variety of plant species. This can lead to a decline in plant diversity and soil health.
- **Alteration of Nutrient Cycling:** Eucalyptus plantations can disrupt the natural nutrient cycles in an ecosystem. Their rapid growth rate leads to high nutrient uptake, potentially depleting soil fertility and affecting other plant species.
- **Water Competition:** As mentioned earlier, eucalyptus trees have high water demands, which can reduce water availability for other plants and aquatic organisms. This can alter the composition of plant and animal communities in the surrounding area.

Water Consumption:

Eucalyptus trees are known for their high water usage. They can significantly lower the water table and alter soil moisture levels. This high water consumption can have detrimental effects on surrounding flora and fauna, particularly in areas already prone to drought.

One of the most significant impacts of eucalyptus plantations is on water resources. Known for their high water consumption, these trees have deep root systems that efficiently extract water from the soil. This can lead to several negative consequences:

- **Groundwater depletion:** In regions with limited water availability, eucalyptus plantations can contribute to the depletion of groundwater levels, affecting both human and ecological systems.
- **Reduced streamflow:** By consuming large amounts of water, eucalyptus can reduce the flow of rivers and streams, impacting aquatic ecosystems and downstream water users.
- **Competition with other vegetation:** Eucalyptus's ability to access water from deep soil layers puts it at a competitive

advantage over other plants, leading to a decline in native vegetation and biodiversity.

In addition to these direct effects, eucalyptus plantations can also influence hydrological processes through changes in soil structure and infiltration rates.While further research is needed to fully understand these complex interactions, it is clear that the water consumption of eucalyptus is a major factor contributing to its environmental impact.

Soil Health:

Eucalyptus plantations have been a subject of both praise and criticism, with a significant focus on their impact on soil health.

Negative Impacts:

- **Nutrient Depletion:** Eucalyptus trees are known for their rapid growth, which requires substantial nutrient uptake from the soil. This can lead to soil nutrient depletion, especially in terms of nitrogen, phosphorus, and potassium.
- **Soil Acidification:** The decomposition of eucalyptus leaves can release acidic compounds, lowering the soil pH. This can negatively affect the availability of essential nutrients for other plants and microorganisms.
- **Reduced Soil Fertility:** Over time, the combination of nutrient depletion and acidification can lead to a decline in overall soil fertility, making it less suitable for agriculture or reforestation with native species.

Positive Aspects (with caveats):

- **Soil Erosion Control:** In some cases, eucalyptus plantations have been used to control soil erosion on degraded lands. However, it's essential to consider the long-term consequences on soil health.
- **Soil Organic Matter:** While eucalyptus litter decomposition can contribute to soil organic matter, the overall impact on soil

fertility depends on various factors, including climate, management practices, and the specific eucalyptus species.

It's important to note that the impact of eucalyptus on soil health varies depending on factors such as soil type, climate, management practices, and the specific eucalyptus species involved. While eucalyptus can provide certain benefits in specific situations, its potential negative effects on soil health warrant careful consideration and management.

Fire Risk:

Eucalyptus trees contain volatile oils that make them highly flammable. In regions prone to wildfires, the presence of eucalyptus can exacerbate fire risks. Their dense stands and rapid growth also contribute to fire intensity and spread, posing challenges for fire management and ecosystem stability.

Economic and Agricultural Impact

Soil Degradation: The high tannin content in eucalyptus leaves can lead to soil acidification, affecting soil health and nutrient availability. This can impact agricultural productivity and the health of native plant species.

Competition with Crops: In some regions, eucalyptus plantations have encroached upon agricultural lands, competing with crops for water and nutrients. This competition can reduce crop yields and affect local farming economies.

Managing the Impact of Eucalyptus

Given the challenges posed by eucalyptus as an invasive species, effective management strategies are essential. Some of the key approaches include:

- **Prevention:** Preventing the further spread of eucalyptus through strict regulations and public awareness campaigns.
- **Early Detection and Rapid Response:** Implementing early warning systems to detect new infestations and promptly initiating control measures.

- **Mechanical Control:** Manual removal of eucalyptus seedlings and saplings can be effective for small-scale infestations.
- **Chemical Control:** The use of herbicides can be considered for larger infestations, but it is important to minimize environmental impacts.
- **Biological Control:** Introducing natural enemies of eucalyptus, such as insects or pathogens, can provide a long-term solution, but careful research and testing are required.
- **Restoration:** Once eucalyptus has been removed, it is crucial to restore the affected area by planting native species to re-establish ecological balance.

Eucalyptus, while offering certain benefits, has also demonstrated a significant capacity to invade and disrupt ecosystems. Its rapid growth, water consumption, and allelopathic effects have made it a challenging species to manage. By understanding the ecological impacts of eucalyptus and implementing effective control measures, it is possible to mitigate its negative effects and promote the restoration of native ecosystems.

It is essential to adopt a holistic approach that considers the specific ecological context and socio-economic factors when addressing eucalyptus-related issues. Collaborative efforts involving government agencies, researchers, and local communities are crucial for developing sustainable and effective management strategies.

CHAPTER XIII

The Need for an Invasive Species Act in India

Introduction

India, a mega-diverse country, is grappling with the increasing threat of invasive alien species (IAS). These non-native organisms, introduced intentionally or unintentionally, have caused significant ecological, economic, and social damages. Unlike many other countries, India lacks a comprehensive and dedicated invasive species control act. This chapter explores the reasons behind this absence and elucidates the potential benefits of such legislation.

The Global Scenario: A Proactive Stance

The global community has recognized the grave implications of invasive species and has responded with legislation to mitigate their impact. The United States, for instance, enacted the National Invasive Species Act in 1996, establishing a framework for preventing the introduction and spread of invasive species. Similarly, the North Texas Invasive Species Act of 2014 provides a more localized approach to managing invasive species within the state. These acts serve as models for other countries to follow.

These legislation typically encompass several key elements:

- **Prevention:** Strict regulations on the importation and transportation of potentially invasive species.
- **Early Detection and Rapid Response:** Mechanisms for early identification and containment of new invasive species.

- **Control and Management:** Strategies for controlling established invasive populations, including physical, chemical, and biological methods.
- **Public Awareness:** Educational campaigns to inform the public about the dangers of invasive species and encourage responsible behavior.
- **Research and Development:** Support for scientific research to understand the biology and ecology of invasive species and develop innovative control methods.
- **Collaboration:** Fostering partnerships between government agencies, research institutions, and stakeholders to address the issue collectively.

India's Gap in Invasive Species Management

Despite the growing threat of invasive species, India has yet to enact a dedicated invasive species control act. Several factors contribute to this absence:

- **Lack of Awareness:** The general public and policymakers are often unaware of the ecological and economic consequences of invasive species.
- **Competing Priorities:** Other environmental challenges, such as pollution, deforestation, and climate change, may take precedence over invasive species management.
- **Institutional Fragmentation:** Responsibility for invasive species management is often divided among multiple government agencies, leading to a lack of coordination and ineffective response.
- **Resource Constraints:** Limited financial resources and human capacity hinder effective implementation of control measures.

Benefits of an Invasive Species Act for India

The enactment of an invasive species act would provide a robust legal framework to address the growing threat posed by these biological invaders. It would offer several benefits:

- **Clear Legal Mandate:** An act would clearly define the roles and responsibilities of different government agencies, promoting better coordination and cooperation.
- **Early Warning System:** It would establish a system for early detection and rapid response to new invasive species, preventing their establishment and spread.
- **Risk Assessment:** A comprehensive risk assessment framework would help prioritize species for management and allocate resources effectively.
- **Public Awareness:** The act would raise public awareness about the dangers of invasive species and encourage citizen participation in control efforts.
- **Research and Development:** Dedicated funding for research on invasive species would lead to the development of innovative control methods.
- **International Cooperation:** An invasive species act would facilitate collaboration with other countries in addressing trans-boundary invasive species issues.
- **Economic Benefits:** By preventing the economic losses caused by invasive species, the act would contribute to sustainable development.

The absence of a dedicated invasive species act in India is a significant gap in the country's environmental governance. Enacting such legislation is crucial for protecting biodiversity, agriculture, and human health. By learning from the experiences of other countries and tailoring the law to India's specific needs, the government can take a proactive approach to managing this growing threat.

CHAPTER XIV

Specific control measures

Each invasive species is unique, with its own set of characteristics and ecological impacts. This means that a one-size-fits-all approach to control is unlikely to be effective. Instead, a multifaceted strategy is required, tailored to the specific species and the ecosystem it has invaded.

For example, an aquatic plant like water hyacinth might respond well to physical removal methods, while a terrestrial weed like lantana might require a combination of chemical control and biological control agents. Understanding the species' biology, its reproductive strategies, and its interactions with the environment is crucial for developing effective control measures.

Additionally, the ecosystem itself plays a role in determining the best approach. A fragile wetland ecosystem might require more cautious and environmentally friendly methods compared to a disturbed agricultural area.

By carefully considering these factors, it is possible to develop targeted control strategies that maximize effectiveness while minimizing negative impacts on the environment.

Here are some common control methods:

Physical Control

- **Manual removal:** This involves physically uprooting or cutting down invasive plants. It is labor-intensive but effective for small-scale infestations.
- **Mechanical control:** Techniques like mowing, cutting, or burning can be used to reduce the plant's reproductive capacity.
- **Habitat manipulation:** Modifying the habitat to create unfavorable conditions for the invasive species, such as flooding

or drying.

Biological Control

- **Introducing natural enemies:** Introducing natural predators, parasites, or diseases to control the invasive population. However, careful assessment and testing are essential to avoid unintended consequences.

Chemical Control

- **Herbicides:** Carefully applied herbicides can effectively control invasive plants, but non-target impacts must be considered.
- **Bioherbicides:** Using plant-based herbicides or pathogens to target specific invasive species.

Prevention and Early Detection

- **Public awareness:** Educating the public about the risks of invasive species and how to prevent their spread.
- **Inspection and quarantine:** Implementing strict regulations for the import of plants and animals to prevent accidental introductions.
- **Early detection and rapid response:** Developing monitoring programs to identify new infestations quickly and respond effectively.

Case Studies

The information was retrieved from Weber (2017), CABI (2022), and Global Invasive Species Database (2022), where the original references can be found.

Species Name	Control measures
Acacia mangium	Uprooting seedlings, cutting trees, and use of herbicides retard growth; triclopyr herbicide mixed with oil used on cuttings.
Ageratina adenophora	Slashing, ploughing, and sowing of other species after removal; herbicides; stem gall fly (Procecidochares utilis), fungus (Passalora ageratinae)
Alternanthera philoxeroides	Repeated leaf removal; herbicides like metsulfuron-methyl, glyphosate, dichlobenil and a mixture of glyphosate and metsulfuron-methyl; biocontrol by flea beetle (Agasicles hygrophila) successful in Australia.
Bidens pilosa	Persistent mowing and hand pulling, prevent germination by mulch; herbicides such as glyphosatetrimesium, xyfluorfen, atrazine, 2,4-D glyphosate, pendimethalin, metribuzin, diuron, paraquat, nicosulfuron and simazine.
Chromolaena odorata	Manual slashing, use of tractors to remove as hand pulling is labour intensive; repeated cutting and burning; chemicals 2,4-D, ester, picloram, imazapyr or 2,4,5-T applied at the seedling stage; triclopyr is the most effective.

Species Name	Control measures
Clidemia hirta	Hand pulling, less soil disturbance, and cuts treated with triclopyr and glyphosate are effective.
Cynodon dactylon	Dug out and remove all rhizomes and stolons; infestation can be controlled by covering with plastic and applying paraquat or glyphosate.
Cytisus scoparius	Slashing, less soil disturbance, pulling out, goats and rabbits stunt growth and prevent regeneration; planting tall and competitive plants may contribute to reducing growth; use of chemicals like picloram, triclopyr, glyphosate, fluroxypyr, and metsulfuron-methyl.
Erigeron karvinskianus	Avoid soil disturbance; herbicide glyphosate, hexazinone, tebuthiuron.
Gymnocoronis spilanthoides	Mechanical removal and hand pulling lead to further spread; herbicides are effective only on the upper part; following herbicide application, the removal with machinery can be effective; dry and burn.
Lantana camara	Mechanical clearing and hand pulling suitable for small areas; periodic burning; cleared areas should be revegetated; use of herbicides- 2,4,-D, MCPA, dicamba, triclopyr, glyphosate or picloram on cuts; well established biological agents: Uroplata girardi, Ophiomyia camarae, Aconophora compressa; integrated approaches are recommended; in India, the control by spraying glyphosate on regenerated growth was effective.

Species Name	Control measures
Leucaena leucocephala	Grazing by goats; solarization was found effective in killing all plants and seeds; pulling out roots and shading leads to seedling mortality; treating of cutting with picloram; cutting stems and treating them with diesel and other chemicals.
Megathyrsus maximus	Pulling out, heavy grazing; herbicides glyphosate prevent new growth; pathogens like Drechslera gigantea, Exserohilum rostratum, and E. longirostratum are highly effective.
Mikania micrantha	Sickle weeding and uprooting prior to seed maturity; slashing or repeated cut from the ground; herbicide like paraquat and 2,4-D amine, glyphosate + picloram; parasitic plant Cuscuta campestris suppresses its growth; rust fungus (Puccinia spegazzinii); increasing shade in forests makes the habitat unsuitable for its growth; potential biological control: Liothrips mikaniae.
Mimosa pigra	Complete digging out; killed by cutting at a depth of 10 cm; slashing and burning with the use of herbicides picloram, hexazinone, dicamba, triclopyr, linuron, and glyphosate; biological control Nesaecrepida infuscate released in Australia; restriction of the movement of vehicles, soil, and sand from infested areas; integratedapproaches are beneficial.
Myriophyllum aquaticum	Biomass removal; cleaning boats; herbicides 2,4-D, diquat, or fluridone can be effective when plants are young; in South Africa, biological control by Lysathia was found effective.

Species Name	Control measures
Parthenium hysterophorus	Manual uprooting before flowering; mowing, slashing, plowing; herbicides 2,4-D, picloram and hexazinone;biocontrol agents: the leaf-feeding beetle Zygogramma bicolorata, the stem-galling moth Epiblema strenuana,the stem-boring beetle Listronotus setosipennis, and the seed-feeding weevil Smicronyx lutulentus.
Pontederia crassipes	Physical or mechanical removal by machine can stop its spread, reduce the nutrient level in the water, chemicals 2,4-D, glyphosate; biological control by Neochetina weevils is effective; use of boom to control the movement of weed; utilization of biomass.
Prosopis juliflora	Control is highly expensive and unsuccessful; mixed mechanical and chemical control; hand pulling effective only on a small scale; stems cut at least 10 cm below ground will not resprout; herbicides: clopyralid, picloram, triclopyr, 2,4-D amine suppress the growth.
Ulex europaeus	Hand pulling and repeated cutting; herbicides: glyphosate, picloram, triclopyr, and 2,4,5-T; prescribed burning; planting native trees and competitive grass suppress growth; intensive grazing by goats; biological control: Sericothrips staphylinus, Exapion ulicis, Tetranychus lintearius; integrated control reduces the spread.

Selected References

Chapter 1 : **An Introduction**

1. Invasive alien plants in South Asia: impact and management by Suneeta Bhatta, Bharat Babu Shrestha, Petr Pysek
2. Richardson etc. 2000 Pysek etc at 2004
3. Richardson et 200 Pysek etc at 2004, Blackburn et at 2011
4. Liu, et d. 2021
5. Disgne et at. 2021
6. Khuroo et at 2021
7. Botanical Survey of India, bsi.gov.in
8. https://www.worldbank.org/en/region/sar/overview retrieved on 5 Jan 2023
9. Inderjit et al. 2018
10. www.indiatimes.com/explainers/news/invasive-alien-species-cost-indian-economy- By Pooja Yadav
11. www.bsienvis.nic.in/database/invasive_alien_species
12. Fatrig L, Effect of Habitat fragmentation on Boidiversity, Annu Rev Ecol Syst 34: 487-515

Chapter 2: **About the Invasive Alien Species**

1. Inderjit & Callaway 2003
2. Invasive Species and Their Impact on Tropical Forests of Central India: A Review, Javid Ahmad Dar, K Subashree, at al.
3. Invasive alien plants in South Asia: Impacts and management Suneeta Bhatta, Bharat Babu Shrestha, Petr Pyšek
4. Mack et al. 2000
5. Khuspe et al. 1982, Nandpuri et al. 1986
6. Kohli et al. 2004

Chapter 3: **Lantana Camara: A Beautiful Invader**

19. H Kato-Noguchi, D Kuradia - Plants,2021 -Allelopathy of Lantana camara as an Invasive Plant, mdpi.com
20. N Priyanka, P K Joshi -Intrnational Journal of Scientfic and Research Publication 3(10), 1-11, 2013- A review of Lantana camara studies in India

Chapter 4: Eupatorium adenophorum (Crofton Weed): An Invasive Threat

21. Meng et al. 2003
22. He & Liu 1990, Zhang et al. 1993

Chapter 5: Parthenium Weed (Congress Grass): A Growing Threat in India

23. Kohli & Rani 1994, Bais et al. 2003
24. Gunaseelan 1987, Morin et al. 2009
25. Maishi et al. 1998, Towers & SubbaRao 1992
26. Kohli *et al.* 1998, Singh *et al.* 2005

Chapter 6: Mikania micrantha: A Growing Threat in Indian Forests

27. A. S. Raghubanshi, L. C. Rai, J. P. Gaur and J. S. Singh, Department of Botany, Banaras Hindu University, Varanasi
28. Tripathi et al. 2012

Chapter 7: Prosopis juliflora: From Helpful Introduction to Invasive Threat

29. Western 1989; Ghazanfar 1996
30. Muthana and Arora 1983
31. Pasiecznik and others, 2001
32. Impact of the Invasive Prosopis julifora on Terrestrial Ecosystems M. Iftikhar Hussain, Ross Shackleton, Ali El-

Keblawy, Luís González, and M. Mar Trigo

Chapter 8: Water Hyacinth (Eichhornia crassipes): A Rapid Invader

33. Yi Z, Zhang MX, Ling B, Xu D & Ye JZ (2006) Inhibitory effects of Lantana camara and its contained phenolic compounds on Eichhornia crassipes growth. Chinese Journal of Applied Ecology 17: 1637–1640.
34. Sun WH, Yu SW, Yang SY, Zhao BW, Yu ZW, Wu HM, Huang SY & Tang CS (1993) Allelochemicals from root exudates of water hyacinth (Eichhornia crassipes). Acta Phytophysiologica Sinica 19: 92–96.

Chapter 9: Chromolaena odorata: An Invasive Menace

35. Inderjit, K. M. Mallik, and F. A. Bazzaz. (2001). Invasive plants: Ecological and agricultural implications. Imperial College Press, London.
36. Liu, X., Guo, Y., and Li, B. (2004). Allelopathic effects of Chromolaena odorata on seed germination and seedling growth of rice. Weed Biology and Management, 4(4), 237-240.

Chapter 10: Ageratum conyzoides: A Troublesome Weed

37. Liu, X., Guo, Y., and Li, B. (2004). Allelopathic effects of Chromolaena odorata on seed germination and seedling growth of rice. Weed Biology and Management, 4(4), 237-240.
38. Kohli RK, Batish DR, Singh HP & Dogra KS (2006) Status, invasiveness and environmental threats of three tropical American invasive weeds (Parthenium hysterophorus L.,
39. Ageratum conyzoides L., Lantana camara L.) in India. Biological Invasions 8: 1501–1510.

Chapter 11: The Touch-Me-Not Plant: A Delicate Invader

40. Soerjani M., Kostermans A. J. G. H., Tjitrosoepomo G. 1987. Weeds of rice in Indonesia. Balai Pustaka. Jakarta.
41. Waterhouse, D.F. & K.R. Norris. 1987. Biological Control. Pacific Prospects. Inkata Press, Melbourne.

Chapter 12: **Eucalyptus: A Double-Edged Sword**

42. Eucalyptus Tree Information - Pros and Cons - 72 Tree Service
43. Effect of Eucalyptus camaldulensis amendment on soil chemical properties, enzymatic activity, Acacia species growth and roots symbioses - ResearchGate
44. Ecological, Economic and Social Effects of Eucalyptus - Food and Agriculture Organization of the United Nations
45. Groundwater Recharge Decrease Replacing Pasture by Eucalyptus Plantation - MDPI , www.mdpi.com
46. Nutrient cycling in age sequences of two Eucalyptus plantation species - ResearchGate , www.researchgate.net.
47. Effect of Eucalyptus camaldulensis amendment on soil chemical properties, enzymatic activity, Acacia species growth and roots symbioses - ResearchGate. www.researchgate.net.

www.ingramcontent.com/pod-product-compliance
Lightning Source LLC
Chambersburg PA
CBHW040130150726

48005CB00015B/2446